MW00791801

The Complete REBT Learning

Whether you're learning how to [...] Therapy (REBT) to work in you [...] use it, this program benefits everyone. Comprised of nine booklets, videos, and workbooks, plus an audiocassette album, this program helps every kind of learner through print, sight, and sound.

For the learner . . .

Learn by reading: REBT booklets
- introduce you to the *ABC*'s of REBT
- help you understand your past actions and how you can turn them around

Learn by seeing and hearing: REBT videos and audiocassettes
- see yourself through others—in real-life situations
- review the videos and audios whenever and wherever you want

Learn by doing: REBT workbooks
- test yourself on the workbooks' questions
- practice and develop the skill of using REBT in your everyday life

For the clinician . . .

A cognitive approach: REBT booklets
- begin the phase of defining the problem
- meet your educational needs for both individual and group sessions

An emotive response: REBT videos and audiocassettes
- provide dramatic vignettes and graphic reminders that reinforce core REBT principles
- facilitate group communication, promoting peer-to-peer learning

A behavioral technique: REBT workbooks
- function as effective assessment and evaluation tools
- provide step-by-step guidelines for client goal-setting and goal achievement

For price and order information, or a free catalog, please call our Telephone Representatives.

HAZELDEN
1-800-328-9000 (Toll-Free U.S. and Canada)
1-651-213-4000 (Outside the U.S. and Canada)
1-651-213-4590 (24-Hour Fax)
www.hazelden.org (World Wide Web on the Internet)

15251 Pleasant Valley Road • P.O. Box 176
Center City, MN 55012-0176

The following titles compose the complete REBT learning program. Each is available in booklet, workbook, audio, and video format:

Understanding • *Anger* • *Perfectionism*
Anxiety and Worry • *Depression* • *Shame*
Grief • *Guilt* • *Self-Esteem*

Rational Emotive Behavior Therapy

Guilt

Revised

Eileen Drilling, M.S.

Hazelden
Center City, Minnesota 55012-0176

©1996, 2002 by Hazelden Foundation
All rights reserved. Published 1996
Second edition 2002
Printed in the United States of America
No portion of this publication may be reproduced in any manner
without the written permission of the publisher

ISBN: 1-56838-959-0

The stories in this booklet are composites of many individuals.
Any similarity to any one person is purely coincidental.

About the booklet
We have feelings of guilt when we think we did something wrong
and regret it. Sometimes these feelings lead to positive changes,
but sometimes they lead to negative results. This booklet explains
how to use guilt most effectively by using the Rational Emotive
Behavior Therapy (REBT) approach, developed by Dr. Albert
Ellis.

   Dr. Ellis, who first articulated Rational-Emotive Therapy
(RET) in the 1950s, changed the name in the 1990s to Rational
Emotive Behavior Therapy (REBT) to more accurately reflect the
role behavior plays in gauging changes in thinking. While the
therapeutic approach remains the same, the pamphlets, workbooks, audios, and videos in this series have been changed to
reflect the updated name.

Introduction

I like to read those colorful, enticing travel brochures. But then I look at how much the trips cost and say, "Maybe next year." Have you ever seen a brochure that said, "Need a vacation? Take a guilt trip." No? Neither have I. Yet it is one trip we've probably all taken at one time or another. (For some of us it's routine, like driving daily to work.) And we are likely to take our guilt trip without a thought about the benefits, costs, time, and energy involved.

So that is what we are going to do in this booklet—look closely at guilt. What is it? What are the costs? What are the benefits, if any?

What is guilt?

Myra is an accountant. She has been stealing money from her employer and "fixing" the books to hide it. In the past six months she has taken enough money to support her gambling addiction. When she got caught and arrested, she rationalized her dishonesty by saying, "My boss has so much money, she doesn't know what to do with it."

Tom lives across town from Myra. Tom's wife had a stroke three months ago. He keeps telling himself he should have stayed home the night she had the stroke. He should have known it would happen. If he had been there, he could have gotten his wife to the hospital sooner.

Tom is feeling guilty. Myra isn't. So what is guilt? Is it helpful or harmful?

The dictionary says "guilt" means feeling responsible or remorseful for offenses. If a person does not take responsibility for past wrongdoings, we could describe that person as antisocial. (Someone who never feels guilt may have an antisocial personality disorder.)

The *ABC* process described in this booklet is based on the work of Dr. Albert Ellis and his Rational Emotive Behavior Therapy.

Since Myra stole her employer's money, guilt would be an appropriate reaction on her part. Had she felt guilty, she might have stopped stealing before she got caught and arrested.

Tom could not have known his wife would have a stroke. He did not do anything wrong by leaving the house that night. To lie awake night after night feeling guilty for his behavior is harmful to Tom. This is "irrational" guilt, although it may be a part of the grief following a loss.

Guilt that pulls down self-esteem or takes away serenity is harmful and inappropriate.

Guilt and shame

We can tell the difference between feelings of guilt and shame by looking at the ways we think about ourselves and

our behavior. If we think that our behavior was wrong and we feel bad about it, we are experiencing guilt. But if we think that our behavior makes us worthless and unfit human beings, then we've crossed the line from guilt to shame. Shame has deeper roots than guilt. It often comes from growing up in a dysfunctional family, a family where we were shamed by adults or abused by them physically or sexually. Shame is chronic, and therapy is often helpful in dealing with it.

A person who is feeling guilt might say, "I'm sorry for

*the way I've acted." A person who is feeling shame
might say, "I'm no good. How can you stand being
around me?"*

Guilt and addiction

Myra has had feelings of shame since childhood. She covered her deep shame with a well-constructed defense system. One of her defenses was to rationalize that her employer didn't need the money she stole. This dishonest thinking kept her from facing the reality of her crime.

Myra served a prison sentence for her embezzlement conviction. While in prison she received help for her alcohol and gambling addictions. She began to understand that she must deal with her shame or she'd never stay in recovery. If she allowed herself to feel shame, she would soon be gambling and drinking again.

Myra also learned that guilt about her past behavior could actually be helpful. If she felt guilty about her behavior, she would be less likely to repeat it.

Coming to grips with the hurt we have caused ourselves or other people by our behavior might prevent us from doing the same thing again. Guilt can help us become responsible. Being responsible is essential to staying in recovery from any addiction.

Making a change by using Rational Emotive Behavior Therapy (REBT)

How can you find out if you are feeling guilt or shame? One way is to listen to your self-talk, that is, the thoughts you have about what is going on around you. If you are telling yourself that your behavior is bad and you need to change it, you are feeling guilt. If you are telling yourself that you are worthless because you have behaved badly, your feeling is shame.

Once you realize what your self-talk is, you can decide if it is harmful or helpful. You can then challenge thoughts that produce harmful guilt.

Look at the following diagram. Notice how self-talk affects feelings and how feelings affect behavior.

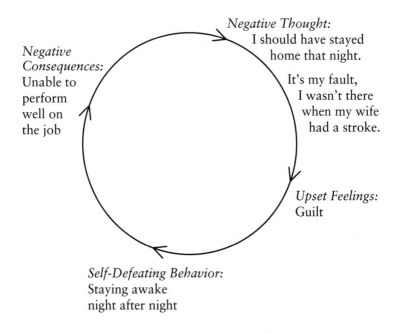

Negative Thought:
I should have stayed home that night.

It's my fault, I wasn't there when my wife had a stroke.

Negative Consequences:
Unable to perform well on the job

Upset Feelings:
Guilt

Self-Defeating Behavior:
Staying awake night after night

Dr. Albert Ellis's Rational Emotive Behavior Therapy (REBT) tells us that what we think can make us upset, and that being upset affects how we act. Tom told himself, "I should have stayed home the night my wife had a stroke. I could have gotten her to the hospital sooner." He ends up feeling guilty in a harmful way. Why? Because his thoughts are irrational. Tom couldn't have known his wife would have a stroke when he went out. He can't change what happened. Tom needs to dispute or challenge his irrational belief that somehow he should have known that his wife would have a stroke that night. If he can do this, he can reduce his guilt and his self-defeating behavior will change. He will sleep again at night.

REBT uses the following process to dispute and change irrational thoughts.

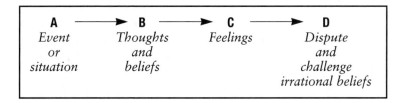

A →	B →	C →	D
Event or situation	*Thoughts and beliefs*	*Feelings*	*Dispute and challenge irrational beliefs*

First, we recall the event or situation that we believe upset us. Then we take a look at our thoughts and beliefs about this situation. Next, we identify the feelings we are experiencing because of these thoughts and beliefs. Finally we try to dispute or challenge the thoughts that are making us upset.

This is how Tom used the four-part REBT process:

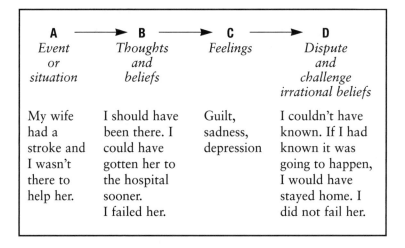

A →	B →	C →	D
Event or situation	*Thoughts and beliefs*	*Feelings*	*Dispute and challenge irrational beliefs*
My wife had a stroke and I wasn't there to help her.	I should have been there. I could have gotten her to the hospital sooner. I failed her.	Guilt, sadness, depression	I couldn't have known. If I had known it was going to happen, I would have stayed home. I did not fail her.

Here's another example of the four-part REBT process:

Jane's mother believes that if her children love her, they will spend every holiday with her. Jane has been invited for Thanksgiving dinner with a new friend she would like to get to know better. She feels guilty because her mother wants her to come home for Thanksgiving.

A →	**B** →	**C** →	**D**
Event or situation	*Thoughts and beliefs*	*Feelings*	*Dispute and challenge irrational beliefs*
I spent Thanksgiving with a friend. Mother is upset that I wasn't there with her.	I'm a bad daughter. I should please my mother. Look at how much she's done for me. How could I leave her alone on Thanksgiving Day?	Guilt, shame	I'm a good daughter. Mother and I are both adults, and we can each make our own decisions about how to spend Thanksgiving. Mother has many friends. She could invite someone else over if I choose not to go. I have a right to spend time with my friends. There is no need for me to feel guilty. I love my mother and I can show this in ways other than being with her on Thanksgiving Day.

Both Jane and Tom had irrational beliefs that kept them feeling guilty. Jane's belief that she must have approval from the important people in her life—in this case, her mother—is a common belief that produces guilt. Tom's irrational belief that he should have been able to see into the future also produced guilt.

Both Tom and Jane put a "should" on themselves. Look for "should" and "must" in your self-talk. When we think we "should" do something, we will feel guilty if we don't do it. It is better to use the words "I prefer" rather than "I should."

Another word to look for in examining self-talk is the word "awful." If we tell ourselves it's "awful" that we did or didn't do something, we will feel guiltier than if we had used the word "unfortunate" or "disappointing."

Another irrational belief that produces guilt is this: I must be perfect at all times and it's awful if I make a mistake. Nobody is perfect. We all make mistakes. Mistakes are wonderful learning experiences.

Guilt and anxiety

After accusing himself of doing something wrong, Marvin feels guilty, and he ends up feeling very anxious. Yesterday he got into an argument with his supervisor. Then he felt guilty and made himself anxious by worrying that he'd get fired. He worried so much that he forgot to lock his office when he left for the evening. Someone broke in and stole his computer. Fortunately, Marvin was able to use the REBT process to reduce his guilt.

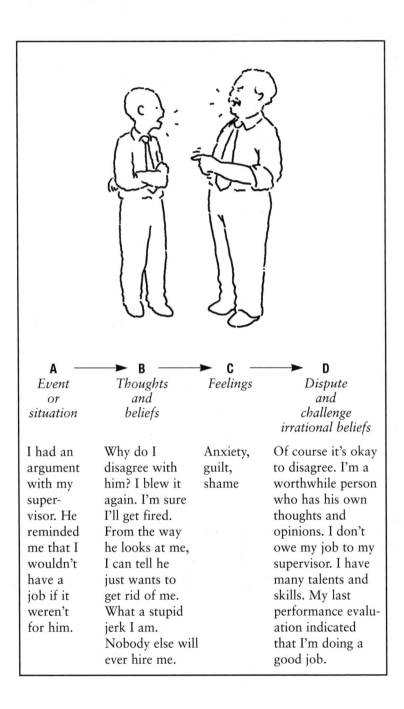

A	B	C	D
Event or situation	*Thoughts and beliefs*	*Feelings*	*Dispute and challenge irrational beliefs*
I had an argument with my super-visor. He reminded me that I wouldn't have a job if it weren't for him.	Why do I disagree with him? I blew it again. I'm sure I'll get fired. From the way he looks at me, I can tell he just wants to get rid of me. What a stupid jerk I am. Nobody else will ever hire me.	Anxiety, guilt, shame	Of course it's okay to disagree. I'm a worthwhile person who has his own thoughts and opinions. I don't owe my job to my supervisor. I have many talents and skills. My last performance evalu-ation indicated that I'm doing a good job.

Notice that one of Marvin's beliefs under *Thoughts and Beliefs* was *What a stupid jerk I am.* Labeling ourselves with negative names is sure to pull down our self-esteem and keep the cycle of guilt in motion. Marvin was able to change this belief to *I'm a worthwhile person who has his own thoughts and opinions.* In this way Marvin affirmed himself.

Affirmations are statements that affirm who you are and build self-esteem. Look at the following set of irrational beliefs. An affirmation that counteracts the irrational belief is given under each belief.

Irrational Belief	*Affirmation*
I should never make a mistake.	I enjoy learning from my experiences.
I should please people or they won't like me.	I feel good when I say what I feel and what I want.
I am bad because I am alcoholic.	I am a good person and I am happy in recovery.
I shouldn't feel angry.	It's okay to feel anger. Anger helps me know when my rights are being invaded. It helps me know when I need to be assertive.
It's my fault that my wife is angry.	I am responsible for my own feelings, and my wife is responsible for her feelings.

Setting a goal and a plan of action

Once we realize we have a habit of making ourselves anxious and guilty, we can set a goal to reduce these negative feelings. Marvin's goal was to reduce his feelings of guilt. His plan of action was to use affirmations. He rewarded himself by putting a dollar in a cookie jar every time he used the REBT process. He taped an affirmation to the jar and read it each time he put in the money. His affirmation read: *I am a happy person. I make good decisions.* Under the affirmation, Marvin put a picture of a set of golf clubs. When he had enough money in the jar, he bought the golf clubs for himself.

You can include your goal and plan of action in your REBT format. Marvin added the following two parts of his REBT process:

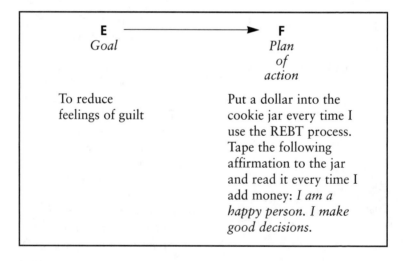

E ⟶	F
Goal	*Plan of action*
To reduce feelings of guilt	Put a dollar into the cookie jar every time I use the REBT process. Tape the following affirmation to the jar and read it every time I add money: *I am a happy person. I make good decisions.*

The REBT process now becomes a six-part process:

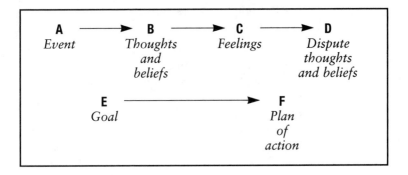

Guilt, perfectionism, and depression

Marian is a perfectionist. Ever since she forgot her husband's birthday, she has been in a pit of depression. She wonders how he can put up with such a forgetful wife. She thinks this way even though her husband has forgotten her birthday several times.

Getting a feeling of satisfaction when we do a job well is not perfectionism. Perfectionism involves more than that; it's feeling uneasy when anything we do is less than perfect, putting unrealistic expectations on others as well as on ourselves, and allowing no room for mistakes.

Guilt and perfectionism go together. Look at Marian's story again. She put the unrealistic expectation on herself that she should never forget a birthday, least of all her husband's. When she forgot, she was plagued with guilt. Here's how Marian used the six-part REBT process to reduce her guilt.

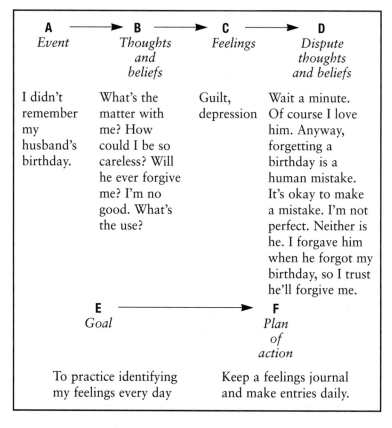

A →	**B** →	**C** →	**D**
Event	*Thoughts and beliefs*	*Feelings*	*Dispute thoughts and beliefs*
I didn't remember my husband's birthday.	What's the matter with me? How could I be so careless? Will he ever forgive me? I'm no good. What's the use?	Guilt, depression	Wait a minute. Of course I love him. Anyway, forgetting a birthday is a human mistake. It's okay to make a mistake. I'm not perfect. Neither is he. I forgave him when he forgot my birthday, so I trust he'll forgive me.

E →	**F**
Goal	*Plan of action*
To practice identifying my feelings every day	Keep a feelings journal and make entries daily.

Marian's story shows how guilt, perfectionism, and depression are related. Through writing in her journal, she will begin to identify her guilt and the depression that results from it. Then she can use the REBT process to find the perfectionistic behavior that gets her upset in the first place.

Not all depression is caused by guilt. Depression can be a reaction to loss or change. This is called "reactive depression." Depression is sometimes biological, that is, it happens because of our biological and chemical makeup. Depression can also be character-related and involves our belief system. Finally, these three kinds of depression can overlap, that is, one's depression might have elements of all three.

Marian's depression is related largely to her irrational beliefs about needing to be perfect. If she can dispute and change these beliefs, she will probably find relief from her depression.

Guilt and anger

Ernest grew up in a family where he was not allowed to express anger. His brother would pick on him and insult him when their parents were not around. When he complained to his mother, she would often tell him what a good, sweet boy he was for putting up with his brother's behavior. This was a payoff for his passive responses. When he reached adulthood, he had formed strong habits of passive behavior. For Ernest, showing anger meant sulking or being moody. But occasionally the pressure got so great that he would really "blow off steam," as he described it. He'd lock himself in the bathroom and hit the walls, complaining bitterly about his wife under his breath.

When he came out, he would have that peaceful look on his face again. But inside he would feel guilty. "I'm a terrible person," he told himself. "How could I get so angry with her?"

Learning to express anger assertively is essential in relationships. Feeling anger is okay. It's a feeling as valid as happiness. Anger alerts us to situations in which our rights are being invaded and helps us know when to be assertive. When we feel anger, there is no need for guilt. However, we may be getting unnecessarily angry because of irrational beliefs. REBT can help us sort this out.

Here's an example. Notice how Ernest's anger changes to guilt.

Ernest is in therapy to learn more about his passive behavior, to find out how it is harmful to him, and to practice assertiveness. Yesterday, Ernest was preoccupied with guilt because he had complained to a co-worker about his wife.

Ernest's therapist asked him to use the REBT process to work this out. This is what Ernest wrote:

A →	B →	C →	D
Event	*Thoughts and beliefs*	*Feelings*	*Dispute thoughts and beliefs*
Maggie and I got into an argument. I couldn't sleep all night. At work, I cornered Ed and complained about Maggie.	Maggie made me so mad. It's really my fault. I shouldn't have argued with her. It's terrible to complain about her behind her back. I'm a lousy husband.	Guilt, shame	My therapist says that Maggie doesn't make me mad. I get upset because of the way I think, such as when I expect her to read my mind, or to think the same way I do about everything. Anyway, feeling anger isn't wrong. It can be helpful. It's all right to disagree. Why should everybody think alike? I'd rather confront Maggie, but it's not terrible to talk to a good friend about my feelings. I love Maggie. I'm a good husband.

Ernest's therapist suggested that he also set a goal (*E*) and a plan of action (*F*), since he has had a habit of passive behavior. Here is what Ernest designed.

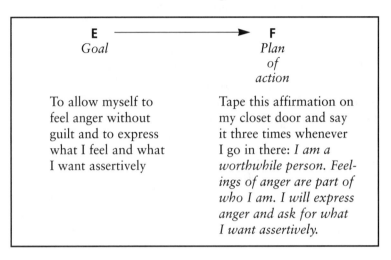

E ——————→	**F**
Goal	*Plan of action*
To allow myself to feel anger without guilt and to express what I feel and what I want assertively	Tape this affirmation on my closet door and say it three times whenever I go in there: *I am a worthwhile person. Feelings of anger are part of who I am. I will express anger and ask for what I want assertively.*

Who's to blame?

When we catch ourselves blaming another person for something, it helps to stop and examine our self-talk. We may

find that we are really feeling guilt, rational or irrational.

Blaming can be a defense against looking at our own behavior. For example, Martha accidentally knocked a teakettle off the stove and chipped it. It was a Christmas gift from her husband's mother. Martha knew her husband would be upset, so she lashed out at him, "Why did you set that teakettle so close to the edge of the stove?

Your mother's really going to be upset with you."

Martha may not even be conscious that her blaming is related to her own guilt, but an exploration of her self-talk just before the incident might help her sort this out.

Summary

Feelings of guilt are helpful when they can stop us from repeating a harmful or addictive behavior. But feelings of guilt can be harmful when irrational beliefs cause the feelings. For example, we may believe that our Higher Power won't like us if we behave in a certain way, or that our parents and friends won't like us if we don't behave the way they want. These irrational beliefs lead us to feel guilt unnecessarily. As adults we need to dispute or challenge these irrational beliefs. One way to challenge our beliefs is to check our own reactions to other's behavior: Do we cut off a friendship if our friend comes to a different conclusion than we do on a topic? Do we sever our relationship with our mother when she decides to spend Christmas in Hawaii rather than with us? Of course not.

The REBT approach can help us get rid of irrational beliefs. Give it a chance. But remember, habits take time to form, and it takes time and practice before we can be rid of them. So practice hard. You'll feel healthier, happier, and more free.